Original title:
The Quasar Chronicles

Copyright © 2025 Creative Arts Management OÜ
All rights reserved.

Author: Giselle Montgomery
ISBN HARDBACK: 978-1-80567-798-7
ISBN PAPERBACK: 978-1-80567-919-6

In the Wake of Supernovae

Stars burst with a pop,
Dancing across the void,
Cosmic confetti falls,
As galaxies get overjoyed.

Planets trip on stardust,
In a slapstick space parade,
Aliens in funny hats,
Laugh as supernovas fade.

Black holes play peekaboo,
With spacetime in a spin,
Asteroids wobble and giggle,
As they make their messy grin.

Comets zip with a wink,
Tail of humor in their flight,
In the wake of the blasts,
The universe feels just right.

Shattered Remnants of Time

Fragments of laughter float,
Like dust in space's bed,
Time takes a funny turn,
As history's seen, misled.

Old comets tell tall tales,
Of journeys far and wide,
With ice cream on their tails,
And stardust as their guide.

Galaxies play charades,
In a twist of cosmic fate,
With each gesture they make,
They leave timelines in a state.

The clock keeps ticking on,
In a wobbly, quirky tune,
Where seconds dance in space,
And giggles fill the room.

Echoing Through the Spiral

Waves of laughter roll,
Through a spiral path so grand,
Stars chuckle in their orbits,
As they twirl and make a stand.

Galactic winds do whisper,
Funny secrets of the night,
While planets share their jokes,
In their disk of twinkling light.

Cosmic echoes bounce along,
In a symphony of glee,
As superstars play hopscotch,
Between the sun and me.

In this spiral dance of joy,
Black holes can't help but grin,
For in the vast expanse of time,
They're the universe's kin.

The Gravity of Dreams

Dreams float on starlight beams,
Where wishes find their way,
In the gravity of giggles,
They bounce and play all day.

Asteroids dream of sweets,
Rolling in sugary skies,
While comets wish for sprinkles,
With laughter in their cries.

Planets hold a silly dance,
Spinning with a chuckle or two,
In the weight of their own spins,
They jiggle like jelly, who knew?

In this cosmic carnival,
Where humor reigns supreme,
The gravity of dreams will hold,
As we laugh and live the dream.

Luminous Pathways

In a galaxy not too far,
Stars play tag, oh so bizarre!
Comets zig and then they zag,
While black holes squeal, they'll never brag.

Aliens dance with glowing sticks,
Selling cosmic space-buffet tricks.
Planets roll like bowling balls,
In this realm where laughter calls.

When Galaxies Collide

Two stars met in a cosmic game,
Slamming together, what a frame!
Explosions laughed, the sky turned red,
While supernovas danced ahead.

Galactic donuts spun in delight,
As meteors rapped in the night.
Asteroids hit a cosmic tune,
And space whales sang to the moon.

Infinity's Embrace

In a realm where time stands still,
A rainbow danced on cosmic hill.
Time travelers trip on their shoes,
 Telling jokes of old-time blues.

A black hole winked, a starlet blushed,
 The universe felt a little rushed.
 Chasing echoes of silly dreams,
 Wrapping light in giggly beams.

Dreaming in Duality

In a dream where shadows play,
Stars debate the silliest way.
One thinks it's time to spin and twirl,
While the other just wants to whirl.

Planets trade hats, a cosmic spree,
Finding humor in infinity.
Twinkling stars share their best puns,
As comets chase, just for the runs.

Celestial Echoes

In the void, a star sneezed loud,
Planets laughed, a cosmic crowd.
Aliens danced on asteroids bright,
Joking about the black hole's bite.

Comets whizzing, like flies in July,
Said the moon, 'I just can't lie!
I saw Mars trip over a ring,
And now Saturn's stuck in a cling!'

Celestial Ballet

Stars twirl in a grand old dance,
Spinning around in a starry trance.
A supernova clumsily fell,
'These moves,' it sighed, 'aren't working well.'

Asteroids laughing, what a sight,
As constellations lost their light.
The Milky Way is quite the floor,
Just don't step on Pluto, he'd roar!

Lost Among the Galaxies

Drifting through the cosmic lanes,
Searching for some celestial gains.
Found a planet made of cheese,
But the aliens begged, 'please don't tease!'

Neptune lost its favorite hat,
Jupiter's mood? A serious spat!
Echoes of laughter, rings around,
In this puzzling space, joy is found.

Shadows of the Celestial Map

Drawing stars with a cosmic pen,
Wishing for some galactic zen.
But shadows giggle, what a fuss,
They scribble lines, and argue thus!

Venus orbits with a playful grin,
While black holes hold secrets within.
The stars roll their eyes at the plight,
In this galactic mess, all is light!

Across the Cosmic Horizon

There's a comet who loves to dance,
With moves that make aliens prance.
He twirls and he whirls, quite a show,
As stardust sprinkles below!

Asteroids join in with delight,
Creating a ruckus all night.
They chat in their cosmic disguise,
While planets just roll their eyes.

Neptune's too cool for this scene,
Sipping starlight in shades of green.
But wait! He throws on a wig,
And joins the fun, dancing a jig!

Through wormholes, they leap and spin,
Grinning cheek to cheek with a win.
Life in space isn't so mundane,
When laughter echoes through the lane!

Oracles of Light

In a nebula's mist, wise old stars,
Tell jokes as they shine from afar.
One claims he's related to the sun,
But everyone knows he's just having fun.

A black hole spouts riddles so deep,
They twist and they turn; we can't help but weep.
"Why can't you finish a game of chess?"
"Because I'm always the one to digest!"

A supernova bursts into laughter,
"Is anyone here a good ghostwriter?"
The cosmic crowd scatters with glee,
As they hunt for the best puns, you see!

The oracles giggle, sharing their light,
Making sense of the dark with delight.
So when you gaze at the stars up above,
Remember, they've all got a sense of love.

Unwritten Constellations

In the night sky, shapes come alive,
A doodle of ducks begins to thrive.
While scribbles of cats lounge without care,
The universe giggles at the flair.

A constellation formed of sandwiches,
Makes everyone crave a nosh in the midst.
"Cosmic hoagie, coming right up!"
Says a starburst, pouring stardust in a cup.

Audacious stars argue about names,
"Should we call this one Lucy or James?"
While meteors zoom, tripping in space,
Bumping and tumbling, they quicken the pace.

In this vast place where chaos collides,
Laughter erupts, and whimsy abides.
So keep gazing at the sprawling sky,
For who knows what laughs may flicker by!

An Odyssey of Light

Through wormholes and spirals, they race with glee,
Space pirates argue about the best tea.
"Earl Grey's a must!" one says with a grin,
While others debate on a stronger spin.

A shooting star strolls in, late to the show,
"I had a detour, but boy, did I glow!"
The cosmos chuckles at tales so grand,
Winking at planets that join the band.

Galactic gardeners plant seeds of fun,
In gardens of black holes, they play and run.
"Watch out for sprouts that might spin out of line,"
"Just prune them with care, and all will be fine!"

With every twist in this stellar delight,
Joy blossoms bright, illuminating the night.
So gather your dreams, let them take flight,
In this odyssey of giggles and light!

Unraveling the Celestial Tapestry

Stars are like socks that mismatch,
Falling from a cosmic hatch.
A supernova sneeze in space,
Turns a black hole into a race.

Galaxies spin like tops in play,
While comets dance and sway away.
Asteroids are just space rock kids,
Playing tag with cosmic grids.

A quasar giggles, bright and bold,
Telling tales that never get old.
Planets grin with their silly moons,
In a waltz to the tune of loony tunes.

In the vastness where laughter resides,
Aliens hold interstellar rides.
With a wink, they zoom and zoom,
Creating chaos from the gloom.

Orbit of Forgotten Realms

Once there was a planet named Fred,
With a crown that it wore on its head.
It wobbled and giggled, a silly sight,
Orbiting stars twinkling with delight.

A moon made of cheese, big and round,
Played hide and seek without a sound.
Comets would laugh as they zoomed by,
Chasing space kittens in a candy sky.

Galactic penguins in space suits bright,
Slide down star slopes, what a sight!
They waddle and tumble, like kids at play,
In a world that spins all night and day.

While black holes munch on space cake treats,
Sucking in all of life's fun feats.
With each cosmic giggle, they create a whirl,
Of laughter and joy, with a swirly twirl.

Radiance of the Infinite

In electric skies where giggles beam,
Light travels fast, or so they seem.
A photon whispers, 'Don't be shy,'
As it rides the waves of a cosmic tie.

Nebulae puff like balloons in flight,
Making jokes in the dead of night.
Stars hold a laugh behind their glow,
While stardust performs in the cosmic show.

The universe hums a silly tune,
To the beat of a bouncing cartoon.
Quasars are jesters, bright and loud,
Tickling the cosmos, drawing a crowd.

From black holes with quirks, to planets that bop,
Space is a dance where silliness won't stop.
So grab your spacesuit, we're off to play,
In the radiant realms where we laugh all day.

Chronicles of Distant Light

Once upon a time in galactic lore,
A star ate spaghetti, wanting more.
While moons played hopscotch on rings of gas,
Shooting stars cheered, 'What a funny class!'

A comet jogged with its swishing tail,
Chasing the meteor through the cosmic trail.
'You can't catch me!' laughed a nearby sun,
As they raced across realms, just having fun.

Aliens chuckled in spaceships bright,
With disco balls shining through the night.
On their radio, a DJ spun,
Jokes from afar, oh what fun!

In the tapestry where humor thrives,
Galactic giggles bring the stars alive.
Join the dance of light and we'll ignite,
A universe filled with comedy's delight.

Celestial Echoes

Once upon a comet's tail,
A space cat told a funny tale.
Of aliens who danced on Mars,
Trading snacks for shiny stars.

They zipped through galaxies with glee,
In rocket ships shaped like a bee.
Sipping soup made from stardust,
While discussing who's the smartest.

One day they found a laughing moon,
That bounced around like a cartoon.
It sang a tune of cosmic fun,
And challenged all to dance and run.

So if you gaze up at the sky,
Remember the cats that zoomed so high.
In every twinkle, every flight,
A giggle waits, shining bright.

Light Beneath the Stars

Underneath the shimmering veil,
Space sloths tell a silly tale.
They munch on meteors for snacks,
While putting on their ninja acts.

Jupiter hosted a karaoke night,
Where aliens danced in sheer delight.
Singing songs from Earth's pop charts,
With groovy moves and wiggly parts.

A starship band played tunes so sweet,
While cosmic critters danced on their feet.
With glitter trails in every spin,
The parades of planets would begin.

So when you view that twinkling light,
Think of all the swaying sprites.
In every shimmer, a chuckle hides,
Beneath the vast, enchanted skies.

Cosmic Whispers

In the cosmos, secrets unfold,
Where even black holes can be quite bold.
They gossip about the sun's new hat,
And how the stars play hide and chat.

Asteroids roll with a cheeky grin,
While UFOs try hard to fit in.
They tell jokes that make comets blush,
And giggle during a cosmic rush.

With space penguins doing the twist,
They whirl through the void, they can't resist.
Swirling dust bunnies dance along,
Creating a stellar, joyful song.

So when the night sky starts to gleam,
Remember it all—a cosmic dream.
For every twinkling light above,
Hides a joke wrapped in starlight love.

Dance of the Distant Suns

Once in a galaxy far away,
Suns gathered for a bright ballet.
They twirled and whirled in cosmic prance,
Creating a stellar, fiery dance.

Nebulas spun in shades so bold,
Each puff of gas a story told.
With colors bright, they'd leap and slide,
What a sight for cosmic pride!

Astro-bunnies hopped from star to star,
Playing hopscotch with the Venus czar.
While Martian frogs croaked a tune,
That made the comets sway to the moon.

So every night, when you wish on a star,
Know there's a festival from afar.
Full of laughter, light, and fun,
In the beautiful dance of distant suns.

Chronicles of Astral Wanderlust

In a rocket built from soda cans,
They zoomed past Saturn with pet plans.
The aliens waved from their disco ball,
Inviting our crew to a spacey hall.

With jellybeans for fuel, they took flight,
Singing tunes that were out of sight.
'Why travel afar when the candy's close?'
Laughed the captain, playing the goofy host.

They danced on comets, twirled on stars,
Pulled pranks on Martians, leaving them in jars.
Each wormhole a portal to giggles and cheer,
In a universe vast, filled with jokes and beer.

Thus, the tales spun under cosmic sun,
Astral journeys turned into goofy fun.
With laughter echoing through the starry skies,
They scribbled funny tales with alien sighs.

Whispers in the Void

In the silence of space, a voice came through,
Said, 'Why did the rocket refuse to woo?'
'It saw a comet with better style,
And jetted away, laughing all the while!'

The stars twinkled, a cosmic giggle,
As asteroids danced to the wacky jiggle.
'The universe is big, but watch your back,
For space cats might give you a silly snack!'

Floating pancakes and syrupy moons,
Tickled by gravity as it tunes.
Black holes yawned with jokes to tell,
While satellites chuckled, 'Ain't life swell?'

In every whisper, a punchline springs,
Even the meteorites wear silly bling.
In the canvas of night, humor is spun,
Wisps of laughter, shining like sun.

Starborne Legacies

With spacewalks that looked more like dance,
They glided through planets, giving fate a chance.
Each orbit a giggle, each spin a cheer,
Galactic clowns made their mark quite clear.

When planets collided in a fizzy show,
They grabbed some popcorn, enjoying the flow.
'Who needs a map when the stars are bright?'
They blurted out jokes, igniting the night.

Supernova parties with cosmic cake,
The infamous aliens sipping on fake.
'We're all made of stardust, but some of us rhyme,
Life's just better when you add a little chime!'

Through ancient tales of space's delight,
They wove quirky legends under the night.
Each starborn heir had a grin, not a frown,
In the kingdom of laughter, they wore the crown.

Rhapsody of the Cosmos

In a galaxy far, where oddballs play,
Planets traded jokes like it's a buffet.
A sunbeam's chuckle lit up the sky,
While moonbeams wiggled, oh my, oh my!

The comets strutted with swaggering grace,
Pulling off stunts in a gravity race.
'What did the asteroid say to the star?'
'You're looking bright, but I'm a bit far!'

Nebulas swirled in colorful hues,
With each twist and turn, they dropped quirky clues.
Life isn't serious, there's joy in the dance,
Every twinkle and wink, a comet's romance.

So gather your chuckles, your wit and your cheer,
Join the cosmic party, with friends far and near.
In a universe where laughter's the key,
The rhapsody echoes, wild and free!

Celestial Cartography

In a map of stars, I drew a cat,
She chased a comet, imagine that!
A pizza-shaped moon, so very bright,
Can we order slices? Oh, what a sight!

With crayons of stardust, I made my way,
Charting the orbits of my wild play.
The Milky Way's more like a milky swirl,
With chocolate rivers and marshmallow twirl.

Planets that bounce like rubber balls,
A solar system with laughable calls.
Orbiting laughter with each silly twist,
In this cosmic giggle, it's hard to resist!

So grab your telescope, peek at the fun,
Celestial antics have only begun!
With aliens dancing, oh what a fray,
In the universe's circus, come join the play!

Odes to the Dark Matter

Oh dark matter, you sneaky sprite,
You hide in shadows, out of our sight.
With your mysterious touch, we often ponder,
Do you play hide and seek or just like to wander?

Floating through space like cosmic fluff,
While we theorize, it's never enough.
Is your home a cloud of invisible mist?
Or are you just shy and really want to exist?

Like a mischievous ghost that tickles our brains,
You run through our thoughts like wide-open trains.
Pulling on galaxies, jokingly tight,
Are you laughing at us from your darkened height?

To the unknown, we raise our glass,
Cheers to the matter that makes science a blast!
In your quizzical dance, our minds take flight,
Dark matter, oh dark matter, you're pure delight!

Lightyear Journeys

Blast off in shoes that are way too tight,
Zooming through galaxies at the speed of light.
My sandwich floats next to a talking star,
Who says, 'At this rate, you won't go far!'

In lightyears, we travel, exploring the night,
Dodging space debris, what a fright!
Asteroids dressed like disco balls,
Dancing to music that endlessly calls.

Coffee cups float in a zero-gravity zone,
While aliens giggle on their weird little phones.
'You've got mail!' says a robot with flair,
It's from Jupiter! Better beware!

With laughter and lightyears, we spread our cheer,
Cosmic adventures are always near.
So strap in tight, it's a wild ride,
Through the universe's fun-filled slide!

Guardians of the Stars

With capes made of stardust, we take our flight,
Guardians of laughter, shining so bright.
We tickle the comets and send them to play,
Bringing smiles to the cosmos, day after day.

Our spaceship's a peanut, and we'm the crew,
Flying through humor, spreading good woo.
The sun winks at us, the moon gives a grin,
In this galaxy giggle, there's no way to win!

Planetary pranks, we're the jesters of space,
With jokes that unravel the fabric of lace.
Stars beam with laughter, as we spin around,
In this cosmic carnival, fun's profound.

So here's to the guardians, with stars as our guide,
Riding through humor on a wild cosmic tide.
With swirls of joy, let our stories unfurl,
In the endless expanse of this funny world!

Songs of Stellar Travels

In space, the stars wear hats too,
They twirl and dance, oh what a view!
With comets that slide on banana peels,
They laugh at gravity, spinning on wheels.

Planets play hide and seek with moons,
Singing silly songs with funny tunes.
Asteroids chuckle, they eat a snack,
While aliens giggle—who's got the knack?

A sunbeam tickles a sleepy cloud,
The stars burst out laughing, oh so loud!
Galaxies swirl in a vibrant spin,
Cosmic cheerleaders, let the fun begin!

Black holes sip juice, a cosmic delight,
With wormholes swirling, they party all night.
Through cosmic jokes, the universe beams,
In this stellar journey, we chase our dreams!

Celestial Whispers

A supernova sneezed, what a sight!
It sparkled and twinkled, pure delight.
The Milky Way giggles, 'Excuse me, please!'
As stardust drifts down like a gentle breeze.

Meteor showers play hopscotch above,
Each one a wish, or maybe a dove.
While suns play catch with comets in tow,
They tumble and giggle, in cosmic show.

Venus wears slippers, looking quite neat,
While Mars does a dance with two left feet.
Neptune's juggling moons, oh what a scene,
As Saturn spins round in his polished ring!

In this humor-filled void, joy is abundant,
Where the stars tell jokes so wonderfully redundant.
From bright exploding bursts to whispers so light,
Cosmic laughter echoes through the endless night!

Starlight Reverie

Stars in pajamas, ready for bed,
Swapping old stories and silly dread.
Galaxies giggle, doing the Macarena,
Quasars compete in a cosmic arena.

Cosmic critters wear glasses to read,
Searching each nebula for the best seed.
Astro-bunnies hop, leaving trails of light,
While meteors tumble, oh, what a sight!

Satellites chat with their friends, oh so bold,
Sharing the latest in gossip retold.
Through starry corridors, laughter will soar,
In this starlight reverie, there's always more!

Rockets amusingly get stuck in a jam,
Whirlwinds of laughter, 'Oh, what a slam!'
From cosmic mimes to traveling jesters,
In the universe's stage, it's all fun and festers!

Echoes of the Cosmos

The cosmos whispers, 'Do the space twist!'
Every planet joins in, they can't resist.
Wormholes giggle as they spin around,
Creating a dance we just can't confound.

Shooting stars steal the spotlight tonight,
Juggling their wishes, what a delight!
In the great expanse, laughter erupts,
As planets play tag and the stardust jumps.

Moons wear silly masks and play charades,
While galaxies chuckle at old escapades.
With supernova fireworks painting the sky,
The cosmos sings harmonies, oh me, oh my!

From black hole banter to light-year leaps,
Echoes of laughter in the cosmos keeps.
In this stellar theater, joy we uncover,
Among celestial beings, laughter and wonder.

Fractals of Existence

In patterns strange and wide,
Tiny galaxies collide.
A cosmic dance, a silly swirl,
Where gravity is just a twirl.

Each star shyly hides its glow,
As asteroids begin to toe.
They laugh and bump, oh what a sight,
In this cosmic waltz of light.

We gaze upon the starlit sky,
Questioning why cows can fly.
With all the cosmos in a daze,
We ponder life in funny ways.

So spiral on, dear space-time friends,
In a loop that never ends.
From black holes to cosmic dust,
Existence is a must-have plus.

The Celestial Tapestry

Woven threads of starlit yarn,
Knit together, soft and warm.
Planets prance with comical grace,
Spinning tales in outer space.

Asteroids wear hats of cheese,
And comets zoom with grace and ease.
The universe, a jester's stage,
Plays a tune for every age.

Galactic quips, a playful jest,
While black holes hold a cosmic fest.
A stellar laugh, a giggle here,
In the cosmos, there's no fear.

So grab your friends, and take a ride,
On celestial waves, with joy as guide.
Each star a wink, each planet sings,
In this quilt of cosmic flings.

Silhouettes in the Nebula

Nebulae swirl in cotton candy,
Spaceships fly, but oh so dandy!
Stars throw shade, they tease and jest,
Making space the best kind of fest.

Planets playing peek-a-boo,
Asteroids wearing hats askew.
In the dark where laughter glows,
Even comets tease their foes.

Birds of space spread silly wings,
Shooting stars shoot out funny things.
In this dance of light and dark,
Silly shadows leave their mark.

So float along on cosmic streams,
As stardust fields fulfill our dreams.
Laughter echoes through the night,
In silhouettes, our hearts take flight.

Celestial Drift

Floating here in space's grip,
Making jokes on a tiny ship.
Gravity's chosen not to cling,
As we invent a cosmic fling.

Black holes joke, 'What's your weight?'
While comets dance on cosmic fate.
We spin and twirl on stardust trails,
In this universe of giggle tales.

Star clusters play hide and seek,
With supernovas, bright and chic.
A cosmic laugh, a comet's grin,
In this drift, we all fit in.

So let us swirl through starry streams,
Chasing laughter and our dreams.
In the night where humor's swift,
We'll find our joy in cosmic drift.

Sparks of the Eventide

Stars giggle, they twinkle bright,
In the cosmic waltz, they dance through night.
A comet sneezes, what a sight,
Leaving trails of laughter in flight.

Planets spin with a jolly cheer,
With moonlight capers, they have no fear.
Asteroids juggle, oh so near,
In this vast show, nothing's unclear.

Light years away, a quasar winks,
With cosmic jokes, it surely thinks.
While black holes ponder how time shrinks,
They chuckle softly, in cosmic kinks.

In a galaxy far, jokes ignite,
As stellar winds spread fun delight.
Watch space-time twist, a merry sight,
In the evening's glow, all feels right.

Nebulae's Dreamscape

In a misty realm where colors blend,
Nebulae giggle, they twist and bend.
With dreams of stardust, they do send,
A shout of joy that knows no end.

Clouds of gas in pastel hues,
Play peek-a-boo with cosmic views.
Dancing stars sing the silliest blues,
As they swap tales like quirky news.

Whirling in spirals, a brilliant show,
The universe teases with a playful glow.
Astrophysicists scratch their heads, though,
As stellar mischief continues to flow.

Through all the chaos, laughter reigns,
In this dreamscape, humor remains.
Stars draw faces in bright terrains,
In the dance of night, joy never wanes.

Halos of the Infinite

Rings of laughter wrap 'round the flare,
As galaxies giggle, a cosmic affair.
Saturn tells jokes; we stop to stare,
His halo spins, a marvel to share.

Galaxies bump like clumsy stars,
In interstellar bars, they drink from jars.
With every toast, they raise their cars,
To infinity, and all its bizarre!

A supernova sneezes, sparks in the air,
While shooting stars crash without a care.
Constellations wink, stirring up flair,
The cosmos chuckles, a wide-open dare.

In this vast playground, oh so grand,
Universal humor plays hand in hand.
Infinite halos, like laughter, expand,
Bringing joy to all, a vibrant band.

The Void's Gentle Caress

In the depths of space, where silence sleeps,
The void teases, its laughter creeps.
Like a ticklish star that boldly leaps,
It coaxes chuckles from cosmic heaps.

Black holes whisper with cheeky grace,
Hiding marbles in a timeless place.
As stars struggle to join the race,
The void is snickering, what a face!

Amongst the shadows, joy can thrive,
Galactic giggles help us survive.
Through stellar hiccups, we all strive,
In the void's arms, we feel so alive.

Space is silly, and time's a jest,
With comets and orbits, it's never a test.
In mystic realms, we're joyously blessed,
As we dance among stars, forever impressed.

A Dance with Nebulae

In a ball of gas and light,
Stars waltz in the night.
They trip on cosmic dust,
In hopes of love, they trust.

Don't step on that black hole,
Or you'll lose all control!
A supernova's a blast,
But don't have too much of a past.

Orbiting in pirouette,
Galaxies make quite a duet.
With every twirl and twist,
Starlight giggles, can't resist!

In this amusing cosmic scene,
Planets play peek-a-boo, so keen.
If you hear a comet's snicker,
Know that it's a twinkling flicker!

Constellation's Lament

Oh, Big Dipper, what a show,
You spill drinks when you glow!
Orion's belt is a bit tight,
His fashion's not quite right.

The Pleiades are a party crew,
But they lost one—they're down to two!
Twirling stars with missing friends,
They'll find him before night ends!

Leo roars with all his might,
But he's just a fluff ball in flight.
"Get off my tail!" he cries in jest,
As Virgo gives him no rest.

A starry brawl, oh what a sight,
When Ursa Major starts a fight!
But laughter fills the void above,
In constellations, there's always love!

Time's Cosmic Weave

Tick-tock goes the cosmic clock,
Time dances like a fickle rock.
Seconds stretch and intertwine,
As moments sip some starlit wine.

Past and future blend and sway,
Quantum leaps lead hearts astray.
"Where'd I leave my time machine?"
"Right by yesterday's ice cream!"

Every hour is a universe,
Some whimsical, and some perverse.
Singularities timed their fun,
While black holes shout, "We're not done!"

Tickling the fabric of the night,
Threads of stars spark pure delight.
With each punch of cosmic fate,
Time giggles, and we await!

Wandering Through Stardust

I wandered through the twinkling glow,
With dandelions in tow.
Stars sprinkled as I danced around,
Each step brought laughter's sound.

Meteor showers dropped by quick,
Tossing wishes like a magic trick.
"Did you catch a falling star?"
"Nope, just my hopes—how bizarre!"

Galaxies swirl in jovial glee,
"Join us!" they shout, wild as can be!
Bouncing through the cosmic brew,
Where stardust tickles like morning dew.

So let's glide on cosmic foam,
In this universe, we're all at home.
For laughter is the light we share,
In the endless cosmic air!

Echoes of Interstellar Dreams

A spaceship lost, not quite on track,
It zoomed past Mars, then came right back.
With aliens laughing, playing a game,
While Earth just watched, a bit of a shame.

Asteroids dance, they twirl and spin,
They bumped our ship, oh where to begin?
A cosmic ballet, a hilarious sight,
As we dodge space rocks, oh what a delight!

Galactic snacks, they taste like gold,
But make you fart, or so I'm told.
Floating in laughter, we sip on our foam,
In galaxies far, far away from home.

With every warp and every jump,
We find new worlds, a cosmic lump.
From black hole burgers to sunbeam fries,
In this vast universe, we're the wise guys!

Starlit Journey

Chasing starlight, we took a ride,
Past nebulae, like a cosmic slide.
Our helmets fog up, breathless with cheer,
As comets pass by, we giggle in fear.

A space dog barks at the moonlit ship,
Getting lost in orbits, we flip and dip.
Alien music, it's all the rage,
A dance party's brewing, we hit the stage!

Rocket fuel smoothies, oh what a mix,
Gave us the giggles, what a fun fix.
Joking with Martians, they float like a breeze,
In zero gravity, they laugh with ease.

We selfie with stars, grab the best shots,
While black holes yawn, in their cosmic knots.
A voyage of laughter, we'll never forget,
In this galaxy wild, we place our bet!

Secrets in the Nebula

In the depths of space, secrets unfold,
Unruly particles with stories untold.
We eavesdrop on comets, with ears wide as saucers,
They gossip about planets, and their ancient courses.

Stardust tickles, an itchy surprise,
As constellations wink with twinkling eyes.
We peek into supernovas, bright explosions roar,
Making a ruckus, oh what's in store?

UFOs fly by, looking quite slick,
Their drivers are squirrels, aren't they a trick?
We wave to the stars, with a chuckle and cheer,
In the nebula's embrace, there's nothing to fear!

So grab your space snacks, and enjoy the ride,
In this funny cosmos, let giggles collide.
Unravel the secrets, spin tales of delight,
As we dance in the cosmos, shining so bright!

Beyond the Cosmic Veil

Behind the veil, what wonders await?
With mashed potato moons and cheese on a plate.
Fish flying by in a bubblegum car,
We laugh as we journey, oh what a bizarre!

Wormholes are so tricky, they twist and they bend,
We pop out in places we thought were the end.
A planet of penguins, in tuxedos they sway,
Inviting us over for a milky way fête!

Dancing with quasars, oh what a thrill,
With stars wearing party hats, they drink with zeal.
A cosmic jam session, the universe sings,
As laughter erupts, and joy brightly flings.

So let's take a leap, through this cosmic delight,
Together we'll laugh, 'til the morning light.
In the depths of space, absurdity reigns,
As we twirl in the stars, holding funny refrains!

Tales from the Stellar Abyss

In the vast void where stars dance,
A comet slips, forgets its pants.
Aliens giggle, pointing with glee,
As they zoom by with cosmic tea.

Rocket ships stuck in a traffic jam,
Drivers all yelling, 'Oh, what's the plan?'
Asteroids roast marshmallows in line,
Making space s'mores, oh how divine!

A black hole spins with a mischievous grin,
Sucking in snacks, much to its chagrin.
Planets play tag, dodging their fate,
But one trips and lands on a space plate.

Galactic parties thrown in a nebula cloud,
With space penguins dancing, feeling so proud.
Who knew the cosmos could be so absurd?
With laughter and stardust, silence is stirred!

Celestial Threads of Destiny

String theory? Nah, it's just a mistake,
Frantically woven by a cosmic snake.
It tangled the stars with laughter and cheer,
Now they can't remember what brought them here.

A cosmic tug-of-war with gravity's might,
Caught in a game that's just out of sight.
The moon calls the sun a big glowing tease,
While the Earth spins, trying to appease.

Every planet tells tales with a quirky twist,
'Remember that time we all laughed at a mist?'
Jupiter's storms throw a wild surprise,
As clouds break apart, revealing blue skies.

In this realm where laughter takes flight,
Even black holes smile, glowing with light.
So let's toast to the cosmic mirth we find,
In the web of the universe, hilariously blind!

Voices Lost Among the Stars

Whispers of comets caught in mid-flight,
Chasing their tails in beams of light.
Starry gossip echoes in the void,
While aliens fumble, feeling overjoyed.

A planet hums a silly old tune,
As meteors dance beneath a bright moon.
Constellations giggle, forming new shapes,
While all the rockets wear funny capes.

Astrological puns ripple through space,
'Why did the star cross the solar race?'
To get to the black hole, oh what a sight!
It's a spin on a joke that's taken flight.

Here in the heavens, where laughter suits,
Planets tell tales, bartering fruits.
So raise up your voices, drift far and wide,
Among the stars, let your true self slide!

Resonance of the Universe

Vibrations echo in cosmic fun,
Galaxies jiggle, and space is spun.
Quasars chuckle in flashes of light,
While orbiting moons have a dance-off at night.

Stars throw a rave, spinning around,
With beats so loud, you could never frown.
Space whales swim with blaring horns,
Swaying to rhythms where laughter's born.

Asteroids play hopscotch on rings of delight,
Hoping they'll land just right in the light.
Even dark matter joins in the fun,
Making shapes in the cosmos, oh what a run!

So let's cherish these echoes, absurd and bright,
In this infinite dance, under starlit night.
For laughter is woven in the fabric of time,
And the universe sings in its own silly rhyme!

Secrets of the Celestial Sea

In cosmic waves, a fish does swim,
With fins of light, and a cheeky grin.
It tells tall tales of stars that dance,
While dodging comets in a playful prance.

A turtle floats with an astroid kite,
Chasing moonbeams in the dead of night.
He whispers secrets of far-off lands,
While space crabs build castles in the sands.

The jellyfish glow, in neon hues,
Joking about spaceport connoisseurs.
With giggles echoing through the void,
They share the laughs that stars enjoyed.

So if you wander through this sea,
Listen for chuckles, wild and free.
The galaxies chuckle, full of cheer,
While cosmic critters draw you near.

Reflections in a Distant Star

A star up high wore a silly hat,
It twinkled bright like a laughing cat.
Winking down at the world below,
It dropped a tune that made worlds glow.

In distant lands, the wise moon said,
'These stars around can lighten your dread.'
But one fell down—a clumsy bling,
And rolled away with a humorous zing.

Planets gathered, a cosmic bash,
Amidst the laughter and vibrant clash.
They shared confessions, funny and bold,
While teasing rocks with stories retold.

When light bends back, what a scene it makes,
With giggles echoing through space's wakes.
Reflections dance, with mirthful sights,
Under the glow of a billion lights.

Beyond the Event Horizon

A daring ship crept close to the brink,
Where spacetime warped and made you think.
With laughter loud, it tested fate,
As black holes opened wide their gate.

The captain wore a sandwich hat,
Claiming it's better than a planet's mat.
He steered through gravity with a grin,
While the crew cheered, 'We will not spin!'

Outrageous aliens jumped aboard,
Danced like stars with a clever chord.
Their quirks defied the cosmic rules,
Making even black holes giggle like fools.

So if you tread beyond the line,
You'll find the funny in the divine.
In swirling chaos, joy can align,
In the heart of the vast, a cosmic sign.

The Language of Light

A photon waved with a giggle bright,
'In wavelengths, my friends, we take flight.
I can shimmy and shake, dance and twist,
In this cosmic rave, none can resist!'

Blues and reds have a banter all night,
Arguing which shade sparkles right.
Their playful jabs shine through the skies,
While mixing colors to disguise.

The spectrum sings a harmonious tune,
While lasers beat like a laugh-filled balloon.
In spectrum fields, all colors unite,
Sharing the joys of the language of light.

So when you gaze at a starry sight,
Remember the silliness woven tight.
For each twinkle tells a tale so grand,
In the galaxy's humor, hand in hand.

Celestial Choreography

In orbiting dance, stars twirl with flair,
A wink from a comet, a giggle to share.
Planets skip hops, with a bounce and a gleam,
While black holes chuckle, causing all to dream.

Asteroids juggle with a mischievous spin,
Every misstep leads to a laugh with a grin.
Nebulas wrap like a funky new coat,
While space whales sing in a retro airboat.

Shooting stars race, all gas and no brakes,
Making wishes for cake and the best cosmic shakes.
Saturn's rings are a dance floor so bright,
Where aliens groove all throughout the night.

So let's join the fun, with a cosmic parade,
In this wild galaxy where happiness played.
For in this vast space, where the giggles ignite,
Even the planets feel cheerful delight.

Threads of Cosmic Fate

In a tapestry woven of stardust and dreams,
The universe giggles, or so it seems.
With threads of mischief, the comets delight,
Unraveling fate as they soar through the night.

Galaxies spin with a whimsical pout,
While asteroids debate what it's all about.
One claims it's chaos, with laughter like thunder,
Another insists it's just silly blunder.

The sun trades its rays for a pair of cool shades,
While moons form a circle, making wacky parades.
They prance through the cosmos, with colors so bright,
Declaring that life is a friendly insight.

So plot out your course with a mischievous wink,
Join the cosmic conclave, it's more fun than you think!
In this woven tale of pure cosmic cheer,
You'll find that laughter brings everyone near.

The Light Between Worlds

In realms where the chuckles eclipse the dark,
A flicker of laughter ignites a bright spark.
Dimensions collide with a wink and a nod,
Creating a ruckus that even gods laud.

Between worlds they share all their quirkiest jokes,
As sprites and fairies exchange silly pokes.
They bounce through the void, with no care in sight,
Trading secrets of wonders that spark pure delight.

When shadows attempt to bring gloom to the day,
The giggles erupt in a luminous array.
With whispers of joy echoing through the haze,
They dance in the twilight, lost in their ways.

So follow the glow of this laughter-filled stream,
Through lands full of jokes as ridiculous as dream.
In between all the worlds where the fun never halts,
You'll find that the light always fosters results.

Luminescent Legacies

When stars leave a trail of their radiant hue,
They tickle the cosmos, as if they just flew.
Galactic gags resonate through the expanse,
As laughter erupts in a cosmic-like dance.

In the chronicles written by comets so fast,
Their glow tells of travels that just might outlast.
A legacy gleeful, stitched in bright beams,
Where laughter expands beyond all seems.

Pulsars are disco balls, spinning with flair,
Beaming a rhythm into the cold air.
The universe twinkles with legacy grand,
Celebrating joy in this wondrous land.

So shine with that light, and let giggles persist,
In the legacy painted with laughter's soft mist.
For in this vast canvas where bright chortles bloom,
You'll find that fun just creates more room.

The Edge of Tomorrow

At dawn, I tripped on a shooting star,
I laughed so hard, forgot we're far.
Dancing on asteroids, what a sight,
Just don't miss your rocket flight!

My coffee's cold, it's lost in space,
It flew away with a wobbly grace.
I guess I'll toast with cosmic dust,
And dream of planets; oh, what a must!

Alien cats wearing silly hats,
Whiskers twitching, chasing space bats.
The universe spins, we can't keep pace,
Who knew that planets dance with grace?

In zero gravity, we all fall up,
Floating popcorn in a cosmic cup.
We laugh at moons, they wobble too,
Tomorrow's edge brings more to view.

Itinerant Stars

Wandering stars with a travel guide,
Making pit stops on a cosmic ride.
They snap some pics through the asteroid belt,
Claiming, 'Look at the milky way melt!'

Just last week, they crashed a space ball,
Danced with comets, had a galactic brawl.
'Why borrow light?' they jokingly said,
'When we can light up the universe instead!'

Alien hitchhikers, thumbs in the air,
Catching rides on a flaring affair.
They giggle at black holes, what a mess,
Where socks go missing, we all confess!

In the end, it's one wild spree,
Traveling stardust, feeling so free.
Bringing laughter from moons that twinkle,
In itinerant dance, we all crinkle!

Guardians of the Galactic Rift

In the rift, a party we host,
Funky aliens, we laugh the most.
Guardians armed with silly little tricks,
Bursting bubbles, we're cosmic comedians' kicks.

With laser beams that tickle and tease,
Protecting space with cosmic ease.
They say, 'Watch out for space-time pranks,'
But we just laugh, giving thanks!

Stardust confetti falls from above,
Dancing with glee, laughter we shove.
Silly hats on our robotic heads,
We play fetch with meteors, nobody dreads.

In this rift, where laughter sings,
We are the guardians of curious things.
So grab your friends, let's take a lift,
To giggles and glee in this cosmic rift!

Songs of Celestial Bodies

The moon sings soft, with a wink and a sway,
While the sun joins in with a bright, bold play.
Jupiter jigs, ringing merrily loud,
While Mars wears headphones, feeling quite proud.

Celestial bodies burst into tune,
Dancing in rhythm beneath a bright moon.
Asteroids tap to the cosmic beat,
As meteors glide, on light feet.

Venus croons sweetly, a serenade rare,
While Saturn spins, giving that flair.
Pluto's joining, though a bit shy,
Singing its heart out with a gleeful sigh.

So gather around, let the starlight guide,
In the symphony vast, let joy be our pride.
Cosmic melodies twirl, through the night,
In songs of the heavens, everybody's delight!

Between Light and Darkness

In the vastness where shadows play,
Stars have a dance, oh what a display!
Black holes giggle, and comets tease,
Gravity's a prankster, just like the breeze.

Aliens laughing with quite a cheer,
Trading their snacks for a can of beer.
Nebulas whisper, 'Join in our fun!'
While planets are waiting for the next pun!

Cosmic jesters in a wacky parade,
Making sure light and dark never fade.
In this sector of giggles galore,
Who knew the void held so much more?

With quasars grinning like Cheshire cats,
And meteors dodging those cosmic spats.
It's a universe filled with laughter and lore,
Between light and the darkness, who could ask for more?

Stardust Chronicles

Once on a star, a big pancake feast,
Where Martians were flipping, not a worry at least.
Space syrup poured down, oh what a sight,
While astronauts danced, floating in flight.

In a black hole cafe, the menu was grand,
Chili that pulls you in, just as it planned.
Jovian hurricanes serving drinks on the side,
With smiles from Jupiter, they'd never hide!

What a riot in this cosmic bazaar,
With stars rolling dice like they're at the bar.
Comets are running a racing o' day,
Zooming past planets, on wild milky ways!

From the bright Milky Way to Andromeda's flair,
These chronicles of stardust are beyond compare.
Who knew space was this silly and bright?
In the stories of stardust, there's always delight!

A Symphony of Planets

In the orchestra of space, the planets align,
Jupiter's bass thumping, oh, how divine!
Mars on the trumpet, giving it a blow,
While Saturn's rings shine with a sparkling glow.

Uranus is waltzing, what a funny sight,
Dancing with Neptune, twirling all night.
Pluto's on tambourine, making quite the noise,
Singing with laughter, oh those space-happy boys!

Venus hits the high notes, sweet as candy,
While Mercury zips by, feeling quite dandy.
A symphony booming across the expanse,
The cosmos is grooving, join in the dance!

What rhythms we find in the voids of space,
With giggles and tunes filling every place.
In this stellar concert of joy and fun,
A symphony of planets for everyone!

Radiance and Ruin

Oh starry skies, with mischief abound,
Radiance flickers, laughter resounds.
That comet's tail, a prank on the sun,
Lighting up space like a jovial run.

The dark side of moons whispers jokes on the breeze,
While asteroids tumble, eager to tease.
In the midst of their beauty, oh what a sight,
Radiance and ruin entertain the night!

A supernova hiccup, exploding in glee,
Galaxies giggling, wild and free.
Boy, when they crash, what a spectacle shows,
A cosmic explosion that nobody knows!

With stardust adorned in shimmering flair,
Space revelers gather without a care.
In this merry chaos, we find the tune,
Of radiance forgotten, beneath a silly moon!

Fragments of a Dying Star

In a cosmic bar, a star took a sip,
Said, "I'm too old for this celestial trip!"
With a flicker and flash, it burst out in cheer,
"You're all invited to my last light year!"

Gravity giggled, and dark matter danced,
While asteroids played, hoping for a chance.
The sun laughed so hard, it almost turned red,
Saying, "You won't leave us! You're better off dead!"

Nebulas joined in, wearing wigs made of dust,
"You can't just go out without a big gust!"
They planned out a party, a supernova bash,
Where the drinks were all fizzy, and snacks went with a crash!

As the star pulsed bright, its glow made a grin,
"Thanks for the memories! Now let's begin!"
With a bang and a laugh, it faded away,
Leaving us all in a cosmic ballet!

Luminous Shadows

In the heart of the void, a shadow did play,
It whispered, "Hey, watch me dance all day!"
Stars rolled their eyes, lit up with delight,
"Looks good, my friend! But you're still out of sight!"

Moonbeams chuckled, they flew past the gloom,
Dancing along like they owned all the room.
"Don't trip on a comet, avoid that bright flare!"
Luminous shadows just twirled without care!

A black hole chimed in with a deep rumbling laugh,
"Your moves are so slick, you should do them in half!"
But shadows just winked and took off in a spin,
"Come join the fun! Where the light never wins!"

So the shadows kept laughing, and light joined the show,
In a twist of fate, they both stole the glow.
In the dance of the void, no one seemed to mind,
A place where bright laughter is blissfully blind!

The Path of Celestial Wanderers

On trails of stardust, the wanderers roam,
With twinkling tales of a shimmering home.
One said, "I'm lost, but that's part of the charm,
The universe hugs me; it keeps me from harm!"

With cosmic maps drawn in spaghetti and cheese,
They charted their journeys with nibbles and ease.
A comet flew by, said, "Join in the fun,
Life's just a journey—so run, run, run!"

Planets played games, tossing moons like a ball,
While giants drank starlight, having a ball.
And as they wandered, with laughter and glee,
They found that the path was a grand jubilee!

So off into space, they twinkled and twirled,
Wanderers delighting in a silly world.
With each cosmic dance, they'd create a new spark,
And tell tales of wonder, deep in the dark!

Guardians of the Cosmic Dawn

Underneath the light of the morning's great rise,
Guardians giggled with twinkling eyes.
Said one, "Let's laugh! The stars need a show,
Let's wake up the universe with a cosmic glow!"

They donned capes of starlight, all shiny and bright,
Pitched a tent made of comets, for a galactic night.
"We'll tell silly stories of meteors' grace,
And tickle the darkness in this vast open space!"

In laughter, they played with the dawn's early hue,
"Step right up, who wants to see something new?"
The asteroids roared—they loved a good jest,
While the planets joined in for an interstellar fest!

With every tickle of light on the wave,
The guardians smiled, feeling bright and brave.
For when darkness loomed, they just shined their way,
Guardians of laughter, in a bright, funny sway!

Songs of the Intergalactic Wind

In the cosmos, winds do sing,
Twirling stars with zany bling,
Jupiter's got a hiccup, oh dear!
Mars hosts a dance party, bring a beer!

Asteroids pirouette through space,
While comets race with a silly face,
Galactic giggles echo so bright,
Creating laughter in the night!

Black holes chuckle, spinning tight,
While aliens joke about their flight,
Cosmic winds play tricks on light,
Giving starlight a comical bite!

So hop on a star and take a ride,
In a universe where fun can't hide,
Laughter floats on cosmic streams,
Tickling the space of funny dreams!

Whispers from the Great Beyond

In the void, whispers play a game,
Saying names that sound the same,
"Hey you!" says the moon with a grin,
What a riot this cosmic spin!

Planets roll dice, take a chance,
Playing tag in a starry dance,
Venus trips over witty remarks,
While black holes steal the cosmic sparks!

Galaxies swirl with gossip galore,
Bantering back and forth, oh what a score!
Nebulas giggle at the shoot of a star,
As they whisper secrets near and far!

So listen closely, the vibe is fun,
In the silence, laughter has begun,
Join the chatter of the stellar crowd,
In a universe where joy is loud!

The Art of Starfall

Stars tumble down like silly sprites,
Dancing through the cosmic nights,
Each one lands with a plop and a splash,
Creating a galaxy-wide bash!

Meteor showers throw a confetti spree,
As they giggle and scream, "Look at me!"
Constellations join in with a laugh,
While black holes prepare for the aftermath!

Planets gather for a starry feast,
Cracking jokes as they munch on yeast,
Supernovae roast marshmallows bright,
Filling the void with pure delight!

So stare at the night and join the fun,
Under the glow of an interstellar run,
For starfall is an art, a cosmic delight,
Laughter and joy take flight every night!

Chronicles of the Cosmic Winds

Winds of space, with tales to tell,
Whisking through stars, casting a spell,
The Sun winks and gives a cheer,
While Saturn spins with a raucous sneer!

Floating on breezes of silly thoughts,
Galactic journeys, tied in knots,
Black holes share a secret dance,
While light-years laugh at fate's romanced chance!

Whirlwinds tickle the tails of comets,
Spinning tales of space-mice and hockets,
Each breeze carries a cosmic jest,
In the universe's silly fest!

So embrace the winds that swirl around,
In every laugh, a joy is found,
Cosmic chronicles hold the key,
To the funniest tales of the galaxy!

The Pulse of Dying Galaxies

In a universe vast, stars pop like corn,
They twinkle and giggle, though slightly worn.
Whispers of comets, oh how they tease,
"Catch us if you can, we're as quick as a breeze!"

Black holes are fussy, they love to suck light,
"Where's everyone gone? I had plans for tonight!"
Galaxies tumble, doing a waltz,
"We're just having fun, don't assign us faults!"

Shooting stars dive, performing their tricks,
"Make a wish real quick, it could be slick!"
Cosmic clowns dance, in nebular haze,
"Want to join our act? It's a stellar craze!"

So toast to the end with a wink and a smile,
For when stars go out, it's a cosmic style.
Dimmed lights lead to laughter, just wait and see,
The pulse of the cosmos is pure jubilee!

Celestial Conversations

Planets gossip, spinning with glee,
"Did you hear Saturn's ring is now three?"
Moons roll their eyes, "That's old news, pal!"
"But have you seen Jupiter? He's looking so swell!"

Stars share their secrets, sparkles to share,
"Did you catch Venus? She dyed her hair!"
Asteroids chuckle, bumping around,
"Watch out big guy, you're losing your ground!"

Galaxies merging, they laugh in delight,
"Group hug, little ones, it's a cosmic night!"
Light years apart, they still find a way,
To keep up the banter, playfully sway.

In this grand theater of twinkling sights,
A cosmic comedy unfolds in the nights.
So grab some popcorn, sit back and enjoy,
These celestial chats are a stellar ploy!

Veils of Extraterrestrial Light

Through filters of laughter, colors collide,
Aliens giggle, in neon they glide.
"What's green and wobbles?" they start with a pun,
"A Martian in yoga, just having some fun!"

Lights in the cosmos, a quirky parade,
Floats made of stardust, whimsically made.
Space cows moo on, in hues of bright blue,
"Why don't we visit? I hear it's a zoo!"

UFOs zipping, they grab some street food,
"What's an alien's favorite? It's a cosmic dude!"
With flavors like joy and a sprinkle of cheer,
They feast on the galaxy, laughter sincere.

In this carnival of cosmic delight,
Veils of bright laughter twinkle through the night.
So dance with the aliens, with sparkles and sass,
In the show of the cosmos, we're all here to pass!

Shadows Cast by Celestial Giants

Watch out for shadows, they're taller than trees,
Celestial giants, laughing in the breeze.
"Who's that peeking?" the starlings all chime,
"It's just the big dude, losing track of time!"

Beams of bright sunlight, they wiggle and sway,
While giants stand idle, taking a play.
"Why so big?" one little star said with a grin,
"Because I'm a giant, let the fun begin!"

Planets play tag, in the giant's long shadow,
"You're it, big buddy!"; they dart like a rhodo.
A cosmic game, just a jovial ruse,
Hiding from shadows is what they all choose.

So here's to the giants, who chuckle and grin,
Casting their shadows, letting laughter in.
In this whimsical dance of the stars up above,
We find joy and fun, a celestial love!

www.ingramcontent.com/pod-product-compliance
Lightning Source LLC
Chambersburg PA
CBHW071830160426
43209CB00003B/263